GUITARS

by Kara L. Laughlin

Published by The Child's World®
1980 Lookout Drive • Mankato, MN 56003-1705
800-599-READ • www.childsworld.com

Design element: Vector memory/Shutterstock.com
Photo credits: AGCuesta/Shutterstockcom: 21 (violin); androniques/Shutterstock.com: 12; Chromakey/
Shutterstock.com: 21 (electric guitar); Dan Kosmayer/Shutterstock.com: 7; Darrin Henry/Shutterstock.
com: 17; interstid/Shutterstock.com: 14; J.Robert Williams/Shutterstock.com: 11; Kamira/Shutterstock.com:
4; nexus 7/Shutterstock.com: 21 (lute); Peter Voronov/Shutterstock.com: 21 (harp); Roxana Gonzalez/
Shutterstock.com: 18; Sergiy1975 /Shutterstock.com: 21 (mandolin); TheHighestQualityImages/
Shutterstock.com: cover, 1, 8; Vereshchagin Dmitry/Shutterstock.com: 21 (banjo)

ISBN: 9781503831933
LCCN: 2018960554

Printed in the United States of America
PA02417

Table *of* Contents

Guitars Are Everywhere!

In a café, a woman sings and plays one. In a music video, two men are playing them. You can see them at the library, at school, or around a campfire. Guitars are everywhere!

❮ *These men are playing their guitars on the street in Havana, Cuba.*

The String Family

The guitar is a string instrument. It makes music when its strings **vibrate**. There are a few ways to get a string to move. A violin uses a bow. A piano uses small hammers. Guitars don't need a bow or hammers. They are plucked or strummed. Guitar players sometimes use a **pick** to pluck the strings.

A pick is also called a plectrum (PLEK-trum).

Picks are most useful during fast songs with lots of notes. ❯

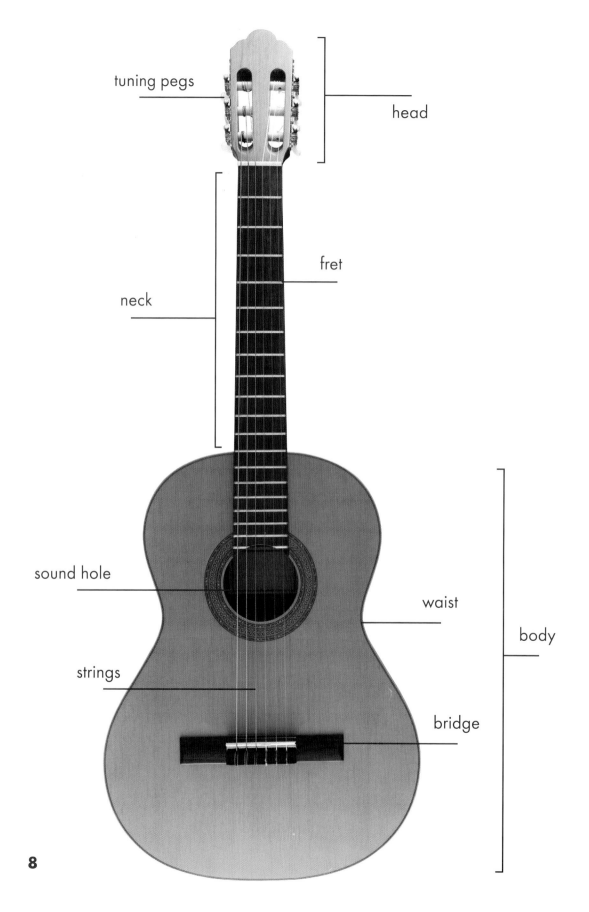

tuning pegs

head

fret

neck

sound hole

waist

body

strings

bridge

8

CHAPTER THREE

Parts of the Guitar

A guitar has three main parts: the **body**, the **neck**, and the **head**.

The body is a curvy wooden box. Its job is to make the sound of the strings louder. Electric guitars don't need a body. An **amplifier** makes them loud. The body is also home to the bridge. The **bridge** is where the strings connect to the body.

There have been guitar-like instruments for at least 3,000 years.

CHAPTER FOUR

The Neck

The neck is the long piece coming off the body. Strings run down the neck. Short bars called **frets** cross it. When all of a string is vibrating, it makes its lowest note. When the string is pressed against a fret, only part of the string vibrates. It makes a higher note. The frets closest to the body make the highest notes.

A person who plays a guitar is called a guitarist.

A player must press down hard on the strings. Pressing too softly won't make the right sound. ❯

EADGBE

CHAPTER FIVE

The Head

The head is the top of the guitar. Here, the strings are wrapped around **tuning pegs**. The pegs turn to tighten the strings. A tight string makes a high note. A loose string makes a low note. The strings are tuned before a guitarist plays.

Gibson, Fender, Epiphone, and Gretsch are all famous guitar-making companies.

❮ *The letters on this guitar are the notes each string plays.*

CHAPTER SIX

The Strings

Most guitars have six strings. Some have twelve. Each of the strings is a different size. Thicker strings make lower notes. Thin strings make high notes. What the string is made of also affects the sound. Many guitar strings are **nylon** or metal. A metal string sounds twangy. A nylon string sounds gentle.

Long ago, guitar strings were made from cow or sheep's intestines.

❮ *You can see the different thicknesses of this guitar's strings.*

CHAPTER SEVEN

Playing a Guitar

You need both hands to play the guitar. One hand presses the frets. The other hand plucks the strings. Some people sit to play. Others stand.

Jimi Hendrix, BB King, Stevie Ray Vaughan, and Sister Rosetta Tharpe were all famous guitarists.

If you are right-handed, you pluck the strings with your right hand. Your left hand presses the frets. ❯

CHAPTER EIGHT

The First Guitars

Stringed, guitar-like instruments have been around for thousands of years. But instruments that began looking more like our modern guitars started being made in Spain in the 1500s. They were small, narrow, and quiet. They had four pairs of strings. In the 1800's guitars got six strings. A man named Antonio de Torres made guitars bigger and louder. Today's guitars look and sound like the ones he made.

❮ *Some people use a strap to help hold the guitar while they play.*

Today guitars are all over the world. They are easy to travel with. They are fun to sing along to. Guitars are used in classical music, jazz, folk, and rock and roll. What kind of song would you play on your guitar?

Other String Instruments

violin

lute

banjo

mandolin

electric guitar

harp

Glossary

amplifier (AMP-lih-fy-ur): An amplifier is a kind of speaker. People often say "amp" for short. Electric guitars can hook up to an amplifier to make them louder.

body (BAH-dee): The hollow part of a guitar is the body. The front of the body vibrates to make the guitar's music louder.

bridge (BRIJ): A place on a guitar's body, usually made of a piece of wood and a piece of plastic or bone, where the guitar's strings connect to the body.

frets (FRETZ): Frets are thin bars across the neck of a guitar. The player presses on the frets to make different notes.

head (HED): The head is the very top part of the guitar where the strings are tuned.

neck (NEK): The neck is the long part of the guitar between the head and the body.

nylon (NY-lon): Nylon is a bendy material a lot like plastic from which guitar strings may be made.

pick (PIK): A pick is a thin piece of plastic, shell, or other material that guitar players hold and use to pluck strings.

tuning pegs (TOON-ing PEGS): Pegs in the head of the guitar that are turned to change the pitch of the string.

vibrate (VY-brayt): To vibrate is to quickly move back and forth a little bit.

To Learn More

IN THE LIBRARY

Landau, Elaine. *Is the Guitar for You?* Minneapolis, MN: Lerner Publications, 2011.

Riggs, Kate. *Making Music: Guitar.* Mankato, MN: Creative Paperbacks, 2014.

Tomsic, Kim. *Guitar Genius: How Les Paul Engineered the Solid-Body Electric Guitar and Rocked the World.* San Francisco, CA: Chronicle Books, 2019.

ON THE WEB

Visit our website for links about guitars:

childsworld.com/links

Note to Parents, Teachers, and Librarians: We routinely verify our Web links to make sure they are safe and active sites. So encourage your readers to check them out!

Index

About the Author

Kara L. Laughlin is an artist and writer who lives in Virginia with her husband, three kids, two guinea pigs, and a dog. She is the author of two dozen nonfiction books for kids.